Why is a relationship with Jesus important?

How do I look up a verse in the Bible?

Find answers to these questions and more at

www.myfaithadventures.com

Copyright © 2024 Allison Reimer
Published by Liberty Alley Publishing

All rights reserved. No part of this book may be used or reproduced in any manner whatsoever without written permission except in the case of brief quotations embodied in critical articles and reviews.

www.myfaithadventures.com

ISBN 978-0-9937852-2-1

Unless otherwise indicated, all Scripture quotations are taken from the Holy Bible, *New International Reader's Version*®, *NIrV*®. Copyright © 1995, 1996, 1998, 2014 by Biblica Inc.® Used by permission. All rights reserved worldwide.

Meet
The Adventure Club!

Meet A.J., Milo, Posey and SATTAR

A.J. and Milo are kids just like you! A.J. is Milo's older brother. He is ten and she is six and a half. Don't forget the half! It is very important to Milo! Milo is in a hurry to grow-up. Posey is the beloved dog of the two siblings. SATTAR (Super-Awesome-Time-Traveling-Automated-Robot) is A.J.'s pet project and friend. A.J. built SATTAR with his dad.

A.J., Milo, Posey and SATTAR have many adventures together. In each one of these adventures, they learn more about who God is and who He created them to be! Join us on these adventures and you, too, will learn more about God and who He created you to be!

Join the Adventure!
Everyday can be an adventure when you follow God.
Spend some time with God everyday. Read the devotions, look up the Bible verses in your own Bible and use the De-Coder Key on page 102 to solve the mystery Bible verses.

KNOW JESUS, KNOW GOD

Yeesh! She did it again. Aunty Marge pinched me on the cheeks. Does she know I'm ten years old now? It always feels weird when she does that. We only see Aunty Marge once every couple of years because she lives far away. Mom says I should give her a chance. She says that if I spend some time getting to know her that I would see how much she really cares about us. So, I decided that this trip I would clear my schedule (video games, reading comics, collecting rocks...) and spend some quality time with Aunty Marge.

In the same way if we spend time with Jesus, we can get to know who God is and how much he cares about us.

Jesus said in the Bible **"If you really know me, you will know my Father also."** John 14:7

We can get to know God by getting to know Jesus better. We can get to know Jesus by reading the Bible everyday! It's really *not* that complicated. Know Jesus, know God!

Well, it turns out that we had a great time with Aunty Marge on her visit. I discovered that she's actually pretty cool! Who knew?! Now I look forward to our next visit.

Join the Adventure!
Read John 14:1-14 in your Bible

WE ARE GOD'S KIDS

Every night when Milo and A.J.'s mom tucks them in to bed, she tells them this: "If you were to line up all the six years old girls in the whole world, and all the ten year old boys in the whole world and tell me that I could pick any one to be my own, I would still choose you!" Every time she says this, it makes Milo and A.J. feel so happy inside to know that their mom and dad love them so much.

The Bible says in 1 John 3:1 **"See what great love the Father has lavished on us, that we should be called children of God! And that is what we are!"** God created you, but more than that, he chose you to be his child because he loved you so much! God is our creator. God is our Father. We are God's children! That should make us all feel special!

Join the adventure!
Look up Galatians 3:26 in your Bible

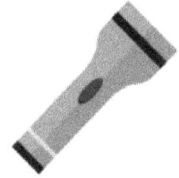

GOD'S LOVE WILL LAST FOREVER

"Hide and Seek!" "No, tag!" "No, HIDE AND SEEK!" "I want TAG!" Milo and her friend Ronan had always played Hide and Seek. It was their all-time favorite game. They always played it when Ronan came over.

Now Ronan said that Hide and Seek was boring and he didn't want to play it anymore. He wanted to play tag now. It made Milo feel sad that she couldn't play her favorite game with Ronan anymore.

There are many things in life that fade away. Some of your favorite toys and games from when you were little have been boxed up and given away because you forgot about them or got too old to play with them.

There is something that *will* last forever, though. 1 Corinthians 13:8 says **"Love will last forever!"**

Some Bible versions say that love never fails! God will always love you! He loves you now when you are young. And he will love you later when you are older. Nothing changes God's love for you. Even when you do things that you know are wrong, he will still love you! His love is forever love! In the meantime, Milo can still play Hide and Seek with A.J., Posey and SATTAR!

Join the adventure!

Look up 1 Corinthians 13:7-8 in your Bible

DON'T DO IT! IT'S NOT WORTH IT

Posey chewed up one of my slippers. She knows she did wrong and now she is hiding from me.

This morning I read about Adam and Eve in the Bible. Genesis chapter 3 tells the story of how God put Adam and Eve, the first two people, in a beautiful garden called Eden. They were allowed to have everything in that garden. Everything, that is, except the fruit from one tree called the tree of the knowledge of good and evil. Read Genesis 2:17

"But you must not eat the fruit from the tree of the knowledge of good and evil. If you do, you will certainly die."

Long story short, they ate the fruit that they were not supposed to touch! Now it says in Genesis 3:8 that they were afraid of God and hid from him. God was supposed to be their friend! The whole purpose of the garden was so they could walk and talk and have fun with God. Now they were scared of him. Boy, I tell you, it's not worth it!

Doing things that are wrong, things you know you are not supposed to do, ruins everything else. Adam and Eve lost out on a lot. They had to leave the garden altogether and it hurt their friendship with God. Good thing God is forgiving! If we ask God to forgive us when we do things that are wrong, he will forgive! Then we don't need to feel afraid to be God's friend! I suppose I should forgive Posey too!

Join the adventure!
Read Genesis chapter 3 in your Bible

GOD'S GIFT TO US

When I woke up this morning there was a new video game controller sitting on my desk! I was confused. Christmas was over. It wasn't my birthday. It wasn't even Valentine's Day yet. When I investigated, I found out that mom and dad had bought it for me. They knew my controller was old and some of the buttons were wearing out. They said they gave it to me because they loved me and knew it would make me happy. Boy did it ever! Later in the day I read this Bible verse from Ephesians 2:8, 9. It says:

"God's grace has saved you because of your faith in Christ. Your salvation doesn't come from anything you do. It is God's gift. It is not based on anything you have done. No one can brag about earning it."

Mom and Dad gave me a great gift today, but God already gave me an even better gift!

Sin separates us from God. But Jesus died on the cross so we could be forgiven of sin. That forgiveness is called our salvation. It means we have been saved from sin's bad effects. We can be close to God again.

This salvation is a gift that God has given to us. We don't earn it by being good. We receive it by believing in Jesus. Now that is a great gift!

Join the adventure!
Take a moment to thank God for the great gift of salvation he has given you

MADE RIGHT WITH GOD

I had a fight with my friend Joely. It sure didn't feel good. I figured she was still mad at me, so I didn't talk to her at school. We just kind of avoided each other in the halls.

I talked to SATTAR about it. He said I should just go and talk to her. Work it out. So that's what I did. I found out that she thought I was mad at her, so she was avoiding me. I thought she was mad at me and I was avoiding her. So really, neither of us was mad anymore. We just thought the other one was. I was so happy when we worked that out. It was like old times. Like nothing had ever come between us.

This is what it is like with us and God when we put our faith in Jesus. Romans 3:22 says, **"We are made right with God by putting our faith in Jesus Christ. This happens to all who believe."**

When we put our faith in Jesus, we are forgiven of all our sin. God does one step better. He makes us right with him. It is like we had never sinned in the first place. Just like there are no hard feelings between Joely and me anymore, there is nothing between us and God. That is what being "made right" means in the Bible.

I'm so glad that Joely and I are friends again. And I am really glad that God and I are friends too – thanks to Jesus!

Join the adventure!
Read Romans 5:10 in your Bible

DE-CODE THIS BIBLE VERSE

Use the de-coder key on page 102 to discover what God has to say to you!

 1:1

GOD DESERVES OUR LOVE

I went to an NHL hockey game with my Dad the other day for the first time. There was some pretty crazy people there! Some had painted their faces to match their team colours, some had crazy hair or hats and some even full out costumes. And whenever their team scored a goal they went all-out crazy. Screaming, yelling, jumping up and down! They loved their team and weren't afraid to show it!

Jesus said in the Bible that the first and greatest commandment is **"Love the Lord your God with all your heart and with all your soul and with all your mind."** Matthew 22:37

God has done so much for us! He gave us life and takes care of our everyday needs. He also blesses us with fun stuff to enjoy like hockey games, toys and friends. And most of all he gave us his son Jesus to die on the cross so we could be forgiven of our sin. That's worth getting excited about! We don't have to act crazy to show God our love, but every day we should remember to send our love God's way. We can remember to say thanks to him for all we have, and obey what he asks us to do in the Bible. This is how we can love God. Oh, and if you feel like jumping up and down and yelling – go ahead! God deserves our praise too!

Join the adventure!
Read Psalm 96:1-4 in your Bible

GOOD MORNING, GOD!

I gotta admit that I was pretty grouchy when I woke up this morning. Mom called several times before I finally dragged myself out of bed. Then when I finally came downstairs for breakfast, I didn't say a word to anyone. I just didn't feel like it. Milo said I was being rude. She was upset that I wouldn't talk to her. I suppose I was rude to her. I was also rude to God. I didn't even say, "Good Morning" to him. After all, God is with me when I wake up in the morning. The Bible says so.

It says in Psalm 139:18, **"When I awake, I am still with you."** Just like it is rude to ignore people when you walk into a room, it is rude to ignore God. God loves us so much and wants to be a part of our lives. We should start the day by saying, "Good Morning!" Ok, I learnt my lesson. From now on, I will talk to God when I wake up in the morning. What about you?

Join the adventure!
Whatever the time it is right now, take a moment to talk to God and tell him that you love him

DON'T JUST HEAR IT, DO IT

Milo built one of her famous tall towers out of connecting blocks. She built it narrow from the bottom up, and tall. She used a chair to place the blocks at the top. The tower was fine as long as everything was calm around it. But then Posey came in from outside. She ran over to see what Milo was doing. With one swish of her tail the whole tower came crashing down! Milo should have built a wider base to support a tower that tall.

Matthew 7:24 says, **"So then, everyone who hears my words and puts them into practice is like a wise man. He builds his house on the rock."**

Jesus told his disciples this story to get the point across that they too needed a good foundation in life. He said there were two men who each built a house. One built his house on a solid foundation of rock and the other built his house on a weak foundation of sand. A storm came and beat against both their houses. The house built on the rock survived, while the house built on the sand fell with a great crash!

Jesus said that whoever listens to his words *and* does what he says to do is wise like the one who built his house on the rock. Hard times or storms come to everyone. When we continue to do what God says to do in the Bible we won't lose out on the good things God has for us because we have a good foundation. SATTAR is going to show Milo how to build a good foundation for her tower.

Join the adventure!

Read Matthew 7:24-27 in your Bible

WE CAN MAKE BEAUTIFUL MUSIC TOGETHER

The other day, my Mom did the craziest thing. Milo and I were fighting with each other, so Mom went into the kitchen cupboards and grabbed a wooden spoon and a pot. I thought I was going to get it, if you know what I mean!

Then Mom went over to our piano and started to bang on the pot with the wooden spoon with one hand, while pounding on the piano keys with the other. Ouch! That awful noise was hurting my ears, so Milo and I begged Mom to stop! Mom stopped making the terrible sounding music, and opened up her Bible. She read Romans 12:16 to us.

"Live in harmony with one another."

Then she explained when a song is written for different instruments to play, the parts are written so that the instruments are in harmony with one another. The different instruments work together to make beautiful sounding music.

God meant for us to live in harmony with one another. Sometimes Milo and I fight because we are so different from each other. We don't get each other, so we fight. Mom explained that when we learn to appreciate the differences of others, we can learn to get along with each other. And when we get along with each other it is like we are an orchestra that is playing in harmony. The result is beautiful music.

So, at the end of it, I realized that I was wrong for participating in the fight with Milo. I said sorry. She said sorry too. Then we prayed for God's help to learn to live in harmony with one another (because, truth be known, sometimes Milo really bugs me!).

Join the adventure!
Read Colossians 3:13 in your Bible

DON'T FORGET TO THANK GOD

Milo was writing a list on a piece of paper. SATTAR was helping her with the words she didn't know how to spell. She was thinking about all the good things that God has given her and she wanted to write them down. She was thinking about how God had helped them get a camper, and about the yummy food they had to eat. She was thinking about all her cousins that she loved and her dog Posey. And most of all, she was thinking about how Jesus died for her on the cross to take the punishment for her sins.

God has done so many good things for us. He deserves our praise and thankfulness! The Bible says in Psalm 100:4 **"Give thanks as you enter the gates of his temple. Give praise as you enter its courtyards. Give thanks to him and praise his name."**

God should be the first and last thing on our minds every day. We should always remember to say "thank you" to him for all the good things he has done for us. Maybe you can write a list of all the good things God has done for you and say "thanks" to God for them!

Join the adventure!

Write down three things that you can say "thank you" to God for

LOVE EVEN WHEN IT IS HARD

"A.J.!" Milo screamed in anger. Up went her hand above her head. She was getting ready to hit him with all the force her little arm could muster up. After all, A.J. had walked by her while she was playing with her dolls and just hit her for no reason. Well, really, he did it because he wanted Milo to play with him but didn't know how to ask. She would be right to hit him back, wouldn't she? A good place to turn to in times like these is the Bible. What does the Bible say we should do when someone hurts us?

Ephesians 4:2 says **"Be patient with each other, making allowance for each other's faults because of your love."**

God tells us that we should remember that no one is perfect. That's what it means to make "allowance for each other's faults." Even though Milo is very mad at A.J. right now, she does still love her brother. She can be patient with him and ask him not to hit her again. Milo just might be surprised by the reaction she gets from her brother. He just might be patient with her too when she messes up!

Join the adventure!

Ask God to help you be patient

DE-CODE THIS BIBLE VERSE

Use the de-coder key on page 102 to discover what God has to say to you!

_ _ _ _ _ _ _ _ _ _

_ _ _ _ _ _ _ _

_ _ _ _ _ _ _ _ _ _

_ _ _ _ _ _ _ _ _

_ _ _ _ _ _ _

_ _ _ _ 3: 16

Once you have decoded it, look up the rest of this verse in your Bible!

GOD ISN'T GOING ANYWHERE

"Sooo, are you holding up that wall? Ha, ha!" My friend Joely is such a tease! The other day at school while I was waiting for her I leaned up against a wall. I was tired, plus she was taking forever to come! I knew I could rely on the wall to hold me up. The wall wasn't going anywhere.

God is like that wall. He isn't going anywhere and we can rely on him! Paul and Timothy were two guys in the Bible who believed in Jesus. They traveled around telling people that they should stop sinning because Jesus died for their sins. Not everyone liked that message so some people tried to kill them. They wrote a letter to the church in a place called Corinth to encourage them. This is what they said about their situation. **"In fact, we expected to die. But as a result, we stopped relying on ourselves and learned to rely only on God, who raises the dead."** This is found in 2 Corinthians 1:9. They figured that if God could raise the dead (remember God raised Jesus from the dead), they could rely on God to help them when people were trying to kill them.

If that's true, then I can rely on God when I have troubles! When a bully at school gives me trouble, I can rely on God to give me the help I need. When my little sister teases me at home I can rely on God to help me keep my cool! No matter what the situation I can rely on God.

Join the adventure!

Read about how Paul and Silas relied on God in Acts 16:16-34

GOD IS LIKE OUR SHADOW

I like to play a game with my friends where we chase each other and try to jump on each other's shadows. It's lots of fun! I have noticed when playing this game is that it is impossible to out-run your own shadow! No matter where you go, or how fast you run, your shadow is always there!

God is like that. The Bible says in Matthew 1:23 - **"The virgin will conceive and give birth to a son, and they will call him Immanuel (which means "God with us")."**

That verse is talking about Jesus! One of the names that he was given meant "God with us." I'm no genius here, but I think the message God was trying to get across to us is pretty obvious. God loves us and he wants to be with us. That is why he sent Jesus! Next time you look at your shadow, remember that God is also with you!

Join the adventure!

The next time you are with some friends play a game of "shadow tag" where you have to touch a players shadow to make them "it". Then tell your friends how God is like our shadow because he is always with us!

FORGIVENESS BRINGS PEACE

Milo was mad at her friend Ronan. They were playing tag at lunch break. Instead of just tagging Milo, he pushed her right down. He didn't mean to hurt Milo. He just got carried away. He had told Milo that he was sorry. But Milo was still mad. When Milo got home from school, her mom saw that Milo was in a grouchy mood, so her mom asked what had happened. Milo told her what had happened at school with Ronan. "It's not the first time he has pushed me down. He just makes me so mad!" Milo exclaimed.

"Let me ask you this question," Milo's mom started, "how do you feel right now?" "Not good!" said Milo. "When someone does something wrong to us, the Bible says that we should forgive them," her mom continued.

"Let's read a verse in the Bible from Ephesians 4:32."

"Be kind and compassionate to one another, forgiving each other, just as in Christ God forgave you."

When we forgive someone, we let go of the wrong thing they have done. We don't think about it over and over again. That only makes us feel more mad. I think that is why you are not feeling very good right now." Milo's mom said. "Sometimes it is hard to forgive someone, especially if they have hurt you before. Forgiveness is the right thing to do though. God will help you do it!" Milo and her mom prayed that God would help Milo to forgive Ronan. Milo felt better. Then they invited Ronan over to play!

Join the adventure!

Read Luke 11:4 in your Bible

LEARN GOD'S MATH

I like math. Sounds crazy, I know! We are learning multiplication at school right now. At church we were learning God's math. They read this Bible verse from Matthew 18:21-22.

"Then Peter came to Him and said, 'Lord, how often shall my brother sin against me, and I forgive him? Up to seven times?' Jesus said to him, 'I do not say to you, up to seven times, but up to seventy times seven.'" To forgive is when you want to make someone pay for the bad thing they did against you, but you don't. You choose to let it go. Peter must have figured that there was a limit to how many times you should forgive someone when they sin against you. He thought seven times would be enough. After seven times surely you can get them back for what they did to you.

Jesus pulled out the multiplication tables when he answered Peter! He said forgive 70 times seven! If you do the math that would be 490 times. That is a lot! Jesus then went on to tell a story of a man who owed his boss a lot of money. The boss forgave the man what he owed. That means he didn't have to pay it back, ever! Then that man met someone that owed him money. He did *not* forgive the man like he had been forgiven. He threw the man in jail! Jesus sums (math pun intended) the story up by saying if we want to be forgiven of our sin by God, we need to forgive others when they sin against us. So, I guess there really is no limit to the number of times we need to forgive! In math terms, that would be infinity!

Join the adventure!

Read Matthew 18:21-35 in your Bible

TRUST GOD AND BE BLESSED

"And please bless all my family, neighbors and friends. Amen!" Each night Milo ended her prayers the same way. She would ask God to bless the people in her life. This is how her mom and dad taught her to pray.

But Milo didn't really know what this word bless meant, so she asked her mom and dad to explain. They started by bringing her to this Bible verse in Psalm 40:4.

"Blessed is the person who trusts in the Lord."

They explained that someone who is blessed is happy. They are not happy because everything in their life is perfect. No one has a life without troubles. This happiness comes from knowing that God loves them, he is with them and that everything will work out in the end because God is on their side.

When Milo prays that God would bless the people in her life, she is asking God to help them find that happiness that comes from knowing God.

Milo understood what her parents had explained to her. "I guess that means I am blessed!" she exclaimed.

Join the adventure!

Pray today that God would bless your family and friends

YOU DON'T DESERVE GRACE

I'm the first one to admit it. I didn't deserve to win. My friend had a laser tag birthday party. That is where you wear a special vest and carry special guns. There is an obstacle course that you can run through. The goal is to accumulate points based on how many people you shoot with your laser gun. You don't want to get hit because that takes away from your total score.

I played well. I got a lot of shots in. But I took a lot of hits! I took so many hits that I am sure it is not possible that I won the game, but I did! I think there was a computer glitch. But they said I won so I got a prize for the highest score. I didn't deserve that prize. That is grace!

Ephesians 2:8 says, **"God's grace has saved you because of your faith in Christ."**

Grace is getting something that we don't deserve. Jesus died on the cross to take the punishment for our sin, not his. That is grace! Our sin makes us an enemy of God because he is perfect and without sin. Even though Jesus never sinned he took the punishment for our sin so we could be made right with God. That is grace! Grace is a gift that God gives to us.

I'm pretty happy that I won that prize for laser tag, even if I didn't deserve it!

Join the adventure!

Read Hebrews 4:16 in your Bible

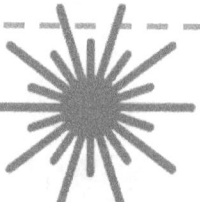

DE-CODE THIS BIBLE VERSE

Use the de-coder key on page 102 to discover what God has to say to you!

GIVE A GENTLE ANSWER

Have you ever had someone yell at you or say something mean? If so, your first reaction might have been to get angry! If mean words make you feel angry, how do you think gentle words might make you feel? Let's see what King Solomon had to say about this in Proverbs 15:1.

"A gentle answer turns anger away. But mean words stir up anger."

The wisdom we find in the Book of Proverbs tells us that gentle words will turn anger away. This means that gentle words will make anger disappear!

Put this wisdom into practice in your life. The next time someone tries to pick a fight with you by using mean words, respond to them with gentle words! When you use gentle words, it will calm their anger and make it disappear.

Key message - God does not want us to react to people in anger when they are angry or mean to us. He wants us to be gentle with people because he knows that gentleness will turn anger away!

Join the adventure!

Read Ephesians 4:32 in your Bible

GOD'S SHRINK RAY

Did you know that God's Word is like a shrink ray? Actually, it is like a disappearing ray, if there is such a thing! Let me show you what I mean.

Let's suppose you are afraid of the dark. You can take your shrink ray, that is God's Word, and blast that fear.

2 Timothy 1:7 says **"God gave us his Spirit. And the Spirit doesn't make us weak and fearful. Instead, the Spirit gives us power and love. He helps us control ourselves."**.

When I feel afraid of the dark I can read this verse in the Bible and say it out loud. When I do that it is like I am blasting that fear with a shrink ray. The fear gets smaller. If I blast that fear with God's Word every time I feel afraid, it will eventually disappear and I won't be afraid of the dark anymore! I know this works because I've tried it!

Go ahead, I dare you to try it. What are you afraid of? Find this Bible verse, learn it and say it as often as you need to. Then watch your fear shrink and disappear!

Join the adventure!

Say this now—I have not been given a spirit of fear. I have been given a spirit of power and love

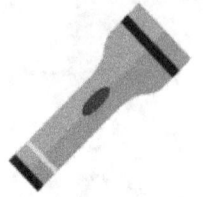

CHASE OUT THE BAD THOUGHTS

I just couldn't help myself. Well, maybe I could have. But it was so much fun to crash up Milo's neat line of cars. My monster truck dominated! There were cars scattered everywhere.

In church we read Colossians 3:15.

"Let the peace that Christ gives rule in your hearts."

I imagined that all of Milo's cars were like the thoughts in our minds. They should be in order, or in other words, at peace. My monster truck was like a big, bad thought that comes crashing into your mind.

A thought like "nobody likes me". If you let it drive around in there it will destroy the peace of Christ in your heart. You need to chase those bad thoughts out of your mind!

A good way to do that is read the Bible. The Bible is full of good stuff to help you have peaceful thoughts. There are so many verses in the Bible like 1 John 4:10 that tell us how God loves us.

If you think nobody likes you, replace the bad thought with thoughts about how God loves you. Milo was mad at me for a bit, but she picked up her police car and chased my monster truck out of town. Together we rebuilt her line up of cars – ready to smash up again!

Join the adventure!
Read 1 John 4:10 in your Bible

CONFIDENT AND BLESSED

I have a favorite blanket. Hey, don't laugh! I bet you do too. My favorite blanket is well used. I have had it for many years. It is thick, soft and heavy. I especially love curling up underneath it in winter when it is colder outside. It makes me feel comfortable, safe and peaceful.

When I say my prayers at night, I always ask God to bless the people in my life. I imagine when I pray this that God is putting a big cozy blanket on them. This blanket makes them feel happy, safe and peaceful even when it is cold outside.

Not everything goes the way we like it in life all the time. Sometimes we have trouble. Read this Bible verse from Jeremiah 17:7.

"But I will bless anyone who trusts in me. I will do good things for the person who depends on me."

Even though we have troubles sometimes, we are still blessed if we trust in God. We can be happy knowing that he loves us, and he is on our side so things will work out in the end! This is what it means to be blessed.

Join the adventure!
Pray today that God would bless your family and friends

OUR FAITH MAKES US RIGHT

Milo had a spelling test at school today. She got 8 out of 10 words right. It was a good test, but not perfect.

The Bible tells us that there are no people that are fully good. We all sin sometimes. Only Jesus was perfect! He is the only one on earth who never sinned. He was righteous! This means that he was completely right with God. Perfect, like a perfect spelling test.

Romans 5:19 says, **"For just as through the disobedience of the one man the many were made sinners, so also through the obedience of the one man the many will be made righteous."**

When Adam sinned, he brought sin into the world. When Jesus died on the cross to take the punishment for our sin, he made everyone who believes in him righteous. This means he made those who put their faith in Jesus right with God. We can be right like a perfect spelling test. This doesn't mean that we never make mistakes and sin again. It just means that our faith makes us righteous or right with God!

Milo's teacher helped Milo learn how to spell the two words she had got wrong. Next time she would get 100% right on the test!

Join the adventure!

Look up 1 John 3:5 in your Bible

COME OUT OF DARKNESS

We had one of those crazy summer wind-storms the other day. The wind was so strong that it knocked the power out. It was nighttime and the darkness was so thick it felt like I could cut it with a knife. I tried using my fingers to open my eyes wider just so I could see a little bit of light.

I gotta confess, it was a bit scary. Milo was so scared that she was clinging to my leg. The more I stared into the darkness, the more scared I felt. Then I found a flashlight. We felt a whole lot better when we switched that light on.

That's the thing about light. Light always overpowers darkness, but darkness cannot overpower light. Jesus said in John 12:46 **"I have come into the world to be its light. So no one who believes in me will stay in darkness."**

When we focus on all the problems we have, it is like staring into darkness. I remember when I didn't want to play soccer because I was afraid that I would let the other team score a goal on me. I was so focused on making a mistake I didn't want to play!

When we look to Jesus for help, he brings light into our lives. I prayed about it and realized that I should just do my best and everything would work out. He helps us to see that even though we have problems, we are not alone. He will help us through anything we are facing. So, the next time you are facing a problem, don't just look at the problem, look to Jesus to find the solution!

Join the adventure!
Look up Deuteronomy 31:6 in your Bible

DE-CODE THIS BIBLE VERSE

Use the de-coder key on page 102 to discover what God has to say to you!

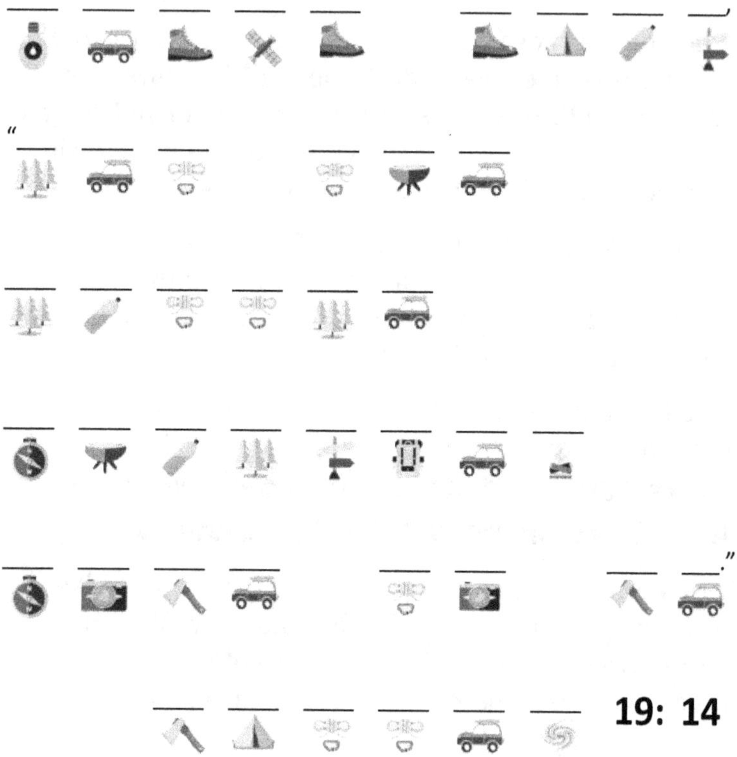

_____ _____ _____ _____ _____   _____ _____ _____ _____

"_____ _____ _____   _____ _____ _____

_____ _____ _____ _____ _____ _____

_____ _____ _____ _____ _____ _____ _____ _____

_____ _____ _____ _____   _____ _____   _____ _____."

_____ _____ _____ _____ _____ _____   19: 14

Once you have decoded it, look up the rest of this verse in your Bible!

HOLY SPIRIT IS OUR CLOSEST FRIEND

I am really close with my family. We love to spend time together. I am even close to Milo! Sure, we fight, but we love each other! I have a best friend too. Her name is Joely. We like a lot of the same things. She likes the same video games as me and she likes to play soccer and jump on the trampoline too.

I am blessed to have some really close friends in my life. But I have a friend that is closer than them all! Can you guess who he is? Let's read this Bible verse from John 14:16-17:

"I will ask the Father. And he will give you another friend to help you and to be with you forever. That friend is the Spirit of truth...He lives with you, and he will be in you."

After Jesus died on the cross and rose again, he spent some time on earth with his disciples. After this time, he went up to heaven to live with God. But he had promised that he would not leave his disciples alone. God sent his Spirit, the Holy Spirit to live inside anyone who believes in Jesus. That is closer than any friend we could have on earth!

The Bible uses different words to describe the Holy Spirit. The one I like the best is "friend". I think that says a lot about who he is and how he helps us. The best part is knowing that the Holy Spirit is always with us, and will be forever!

Join the adventure!

Read John 14:26 in your Bible

GRACE IS A GIFT FROM GOD

Normally Milo would be expected to eat her whole supper, especially her vegetables before she would be allowed to have dessert. Today, was a special day, however. It was the birthday of Milo and A.J.'s Grandpa. Her grandparents had come over for supper and birthday cake. Everyone was ready for the cake except for Milo. She had not finished the veggies on her plate. Today, Milo's mom made an exception and allowed her to have cake with the rest of the family.

That is grace! Grace is getting something that you don't deserve. The expectation in Milo's household was that she finish her veggies before dessert but today she received grace and was allowed to have cake even though she didn't finish them.

Romans 3:24 says, **"The free gift of God's grace makes us right with him."**

Grace is a word that is used in the Bible a lot. God showed us grace when he gave his Son Jesus to die for our sins even though we did not deserve it. The Bible says we were enemies of God because of our sin. Even though we were God's enemies he gave us Jesus. That is grace!

Join the adventure!

Read John 1:16-17 in your Bible

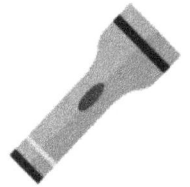

YOU CAN TRUST GOD

Milo was always asking "why". She had to understand everything. When her mom asked her to wash her hands, Milo would ask "why". When her dad said it was time for bed, Milo would ask "why". When A.J. would ask her to play with him, Milo would ask "why".

One day Milo's mom asked Milo to get ready to go out. Of course, Milo asked "why". Milo wanted to know where they were going. Milo's mom just told her that Milo would have to trust her and that she would find out soon enough.

Milo was a little bit worried. "Maybe Mom wants to take me to the doctor for a needle," she thought to herself. Milo thought about it for a bit. Her mom would tell her about something like that. She could trust her mom. Her mom had never done anything to deceive Milo before.

Proverbs 3:5 and 6 says, **"Trust in the Lord with all your heart. Do not depend on your own understanding. In all your ways obey him. Then he will make your paths smooth and straight."**

Milo was confident that her mom was good and had her best in mind. The Bible says we can trust God like this too! We can be confident that God always has our best in mind even when we don't understand what he is asking us to do. We can trust God.

Milo found out later that her mom and dad were taking her and A.J. out for ice cream. It was meant to be a surprise. Milo knew she could trust her mom!

Join the adventure!

Read 2 Corinthians 5:7 in your Bible

GOD HAS SUPER-SONIC HEARING

My neighbor Joely came over to play today. Milo and I decided to play a little trick on her. We pretended to talk to each other and Joely, but there was no sound coming out of our mouths! We made Joely think that her ears weren't working right. Finally, we told her what we were doing, and we all had a good laugh.

Later Joely asked me if I thought that God knew what we were saying. I told her that God has super-sonic hearing! He can hear anything – even what goes on in our heads! When we put our trust in Jesus, God's Spirit, also called the Holy Spirit, comes to live in our hearts.

The Bible says in Romans 8:27 **"And he who searches our hearts knows the mind of the Spirit."**

God searches our hearts. God knows all our thoughts because he searches our hearts through the Holy Spirit who lives in us. God can hear us when we whisper. God also knows all our thoughts! So, we can pray in our hearts, without sound, and God can still hear us. Now that is super-sonic hearing!

Join the adventure!

Read Matthew 6:6-8 in your Bible

LIVE UNDER HOLY SPIRIT'S CONTROL

True confessions – when I was younger, I stole candy from the corner store. I was passing by the store on the way home from school one day. I didn't have any money and I really wanted some candy! I stood outside the store and struggled with my thoughts.

"Should I steal the candy? I shouldn't steal the candy because stealing is wrong. But I really want the candy! The Bible says we shouldn't steal. I will be quick. No one will know."

Eventually, I went inside the store and I stole the candy. And then I ate the candy.

Romans 8:4 says, **"The power of sin should no longer control the way we live. The Holy Spirit should control the way we live."**

Sin was definitely controlling the way that I was living that day that I stole the candy! I knew what the Bible says about stealing, but I chose to sin anyway. I should have listened to what the Holy Spirit was saying to me. It was the Holy Spirit inside of me that was trying to tell me to not steal the candy. That day, I let sin have the control, and not the Holy Spirit.

I felt really bad after that. I didn't tell anyone for a few days. Those days were bad. I did not feel good inside. Finally, I told my mom and we went to the store together to apologize and pay for the candy. That day I let the Holy Spirit have the control. I felt a whole lot better after that!

Join the adventure!

Say this—I am not controlled by sin.
I am controlled by Holy Spirit.

SAY NICE THINGS TO YOURSELF

Did you know that you are always thinking? You can never turn your thoughts off! When you are thinking it is like you are talking to yourself inside your head.

The other day Milo came home from school with these thoughts in her head. "I'm ugly". A boy at school had pulled her hair and said those words to her. She started to think about those hurtful words and started to think that she was ugly! This made Milo feel very sad.

The Bible says in Phillippians 4:8 **"Whatever is true... whatever is right...whatever is good - think on these things."**

We need to say nice things to ourselves when we are thinking, not mean things! The Bible says that God made us wonderful, not ugly! We can't control what other people say to us, but we can control what we say to ourselves when we are thinking. Say nice things to yourself!

Join the adventure!

Say this Bible verse to yourself—"I am made in the image of God!" Now look up Genesis 1:27

DE-CODE THIS BIBLE VERSE

Use the de-coder key on page 102 to discover what God has to say to you!

Read the rest of this verse in your Bible!

1 ___ ___ ___ ___ 4: 7

SPEAK THE TRUTH

To learn about the life cycle of birds, Milo's class at school got a baby chick. Milo and her classmates were responsible to keep the little chick's cage clean. Today was Milo's turn. Milo was trying to remove the dirty shavings from the cage, but the little chick kept getting in the way. Milo could not control that little chick! So, Milo decided to tell her teacher that she had finished cleaning the cage, even though she hadn't. That was a lie!

Later, when Mrs. Garba checked the cage, she could clearly see that the cage had not been cleaned. Milo's lie had been discovered! Mrs. Garba asked Milo why she had lied. Milo explained how she could not control the little chick and it kept getting in the way. Mrs. Garba shared a verse from the Bible with Milo. In Ephesians 4:25 it says, **"So each of you must get rid of your lying. Speak the truth to your neighbor."**

Mrs. Garba explained that this verse means we can control whether we tell lies or not, even if we can't control a little baby chick! Milo was sorry she had lied and asked Mrs. Garba to forgive her. Mrs. Garba forgave Milo and helped her with that little chick while Milo finished cleaning the cage!

Join the adventure!

Read John 14:6 in your Bible

CONTROL YOUR LIPS

I told a lie at school the other day. I was in a panic! I didn't know what to do. I couldn't use the "dog ate my homework" excuse. I hadn't finished my science project that was due. The truth is, I was too busy playing and I forgot to finish. But I told Mr. Barton that my sister, Milo, had spilled paint on my project so I needed more time to finish. Only problem is, Milo goes to the same school as me! Mr. Barton saw Milo in the hall and asked what she had been painting when the paint spilled on my project – I was busted!

Mr. Barton gave more time to finish my project – but I was automatically losing 10 marks for it being late, *and* I had extra classroom cleaning duties as a consequence for lying to Mr. Barton. I felt really bad for lying, too. I don't think Mr. Barton is going to trust me as much the next time I am late for a project. It is true what the Bible says – **"If you want to have good days, keep your lips from telling lies"** (Psalm 34:12,13). The last few days weren't very good at school. I think from now on I will follow the advice from the Bible and keep my lips from telling lies!

Join the adventure!

Read John 8:31-32 in your Bible

I CAN DO ALL THROUGH JESUS

The Bible tells us a lot about a great man of faith named Moses. He was the guy that God used to split the Red Sea apart so the Israelites could escape Egypt. Did you know that when God first called Moses, he did not respond with faith? If you read Exodus chapter 3, you will see that when God first asked Moses to approach Pharaoh, he said, "Who me? I can't do that!"

Moses had a whole bunch of excuses as to why he couldn't help God out. God told him, "If I have asked you to do it, I will help you to do it."

That is what God is saying to us today in this Bible verse from Philippians 4:13.

"I can do all this by the power of Christ. He gives me strength."

God isn't saying here that we can be like a super-hero and leap tall buildings in a single bound. He is telling us that whatever he asks us to do, he will help us do it!

He will help us do our best at school and get good grades.

He will help us obey our parents and have a good relationship with them.

He will help us show God's love to people who are not being so nice to us.

He will help us share the good news about Jesus wherever we go.

Life can have challenges. Whenever we are faced with those challenges, we can make this our Faith Confession - "I can do all things through Jesus who gives me strength."

If you are struggling to understand something at school, say this - "I can do all things through Jesus who gives me strength." If you feel you should tell a friend about Jesus, but are scared, say this - "I can do all things through Jesus who gives me strength." Whatever your challenge may be, if God has asked you to do it, God will help you do it!

Join the adventure!

Read the story of Moses in Exodus chapter 3

I can do All Things Through Jesus!

HIKE ON THE NARROW PATH

We have some great hiking trails not too far from our house. I love hiking them because there are a lot of rocks to climb. The path is narrow so Dad usually goes in front, then me and Milo followed by Mom. Posey usually runs through the bush! We could find an easier place to take a walk, I suppose. Something wider and flat. It would be easier, but not as much fun!

Sometimes I look at life like it is a hiking path. Matthew 7:13 says, **"Enter through the narrow gate. For wide is the gate and broad is the road that leads to destruction, and many enter through it. But small is the gate and narrow the road that leads to life, and only a few find it."**

The path that leads to the great life God has for us is narrow. It means doing what God says even when it is hard. Like when a friend wants you to look at something on their phone that you know is wrong. They may make fun of you for saying no, but that is the choice that leads to life. Choosing against God leads to destruction. So many people choose to disobey God because it is easier. But that leads to destruction. I choose take a hike on the narrow path!

Join the adventure!

Read Psalm 25:4 in your Bible

THE HEAVENS DECLARE

A.J. and Milo were allowed to stay home from school today so they could watch the total solar eclipse. SATTAR explained to them that a total solar eclipse occurs when the moon passes directly in front of the sun during the day blocking its light. So with their special glasses to protect their eyes, A.J. and Milo were able to watch the spectacular event! When the moon was directly in front of the sun, the sky got dark and there was a bright orange ring shining around the moon. The air temperature even got cooler when the moon was in front of the sun. It was amazing! While they were watching, SATTAR read this Bible verse from Psalm 19:1.

"The heavens tell about the glory of God. The skies show that his hands created them."

SATTAR then explained that you can see God's handiwork in all of creation. "Everything we see from the stars to planets, plants to animals, people and everything in between was perfectly designed and made by God."

"Wow," said Milo. "When you think about all that God has made you realize just how awesome and powerful he is!"

After the eclipse had passed, A.J., Milo and SATTAR went on a walk in the forest to look at all the other amazing things God had created for them to enjoy.

Join the adventure!
Read Romans 1:20 in your Bible

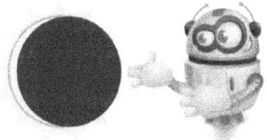

HEALED BY JESUS

Milo did not get sick very often and did not miss school very easily. She loved school and hated to miss it. But today Milo had to stay home. She had a sore throat, a runny nose and a fever. Milo was upset. She did not like to be sick and she did not like to miss school.

Milo had received a Faith Confession card at church that said – "I am healed by the wounds of Jesus." It was based on the Bible verse from 1 Peter 2:24.

" 'He himself carried our sins' in his body on the cross. He did it so that we would die as far as sins are concerned. Then we would lead godly lives. 'His wounds have healed you.' "

When Jesus died on the cross, he took our sin away *and* he took our sickness away! The wounds that Jesus suffered on the cross have healed us too. That is why we can say "I am healed by the wounds of Jesus" when we do not feel well.

So that is what Milo did. She rested on the couch and thanked God that she had been healed by the wounds of Jesus. By the end of the day, Milo was feeling so much better. The next day she was able to go back to school!

Join the adventure!

The next time you are sick say this—
I am healed by the wounds of Jesus

DE-CODE THIS BIBLE VERSE

Use the de-coder key on page 102 to discover what God has to say to you!

Read the rest of this verse in your Bible!

THERE IS ALWAYS A REASON TO GIVE THANKS

It was the deciding game. If we won this soccer game, we would advance to the play-offs. We had worked so hard all year and had come so far. The game was tied, but in the last 15 minutes of the second half, the other team scored. We never came back after that and lost the game! The season was over for us. We were all devastated!

We went back to the locker room to change. Some of us were just quiet. We sat there with our heads hanging down. Others were complaining that the linesmen made some bad calls. Some were talking about quitting and not playing soccer anymore. It was understandable that we were feeling so disappointed.

Coach stopped us. He told us that we needed to put things into perspective. That means we weren't looking at the whole picture. He read a Bible verse from 1 Thessalonians 5:18 to us.

"Give thanks no matter what happens."

He said that we were only focusing on the bad thing that happened – losing the big game. We were forgetting about all the things that we had to be thankful for. No one on the team got injured at all during the season. We played better than last year and learned new skills. We had a fun time hanging out with each other during the season. We even got to go on a fun road trip for a tournament. And, we also had the chance to play again next season.

Coach explained that even though losing the game was a big disappointment, we could still give thanks to God for all the good things that we had to be grateful for. Even during the hardest times in life, there is always something that we can give thanks to God for.

Join the adventure!

Stop right now and think of something to thank God for

HAVE FAITH WHEN YOU PRAY

A.J. was saving up his money for a new video game. Some of his friends already had it. They were all planning on playing online together on the weekend and A.J. really wanted to be a part of it, but he didn't have the game yet. He was $10 short of being able to buy it.

He had asked his parents if he could just borrow the money from them and pay them back. But they had a rule that A.J. could earn his own money to spend on the games he likes. Borrowing money for such things was not a good habit to make.

Rather than borrow the money, they suggested that A.J. ask God to provide the money that he needed. They read Mark 11:24 with A.J.

"So, I tell you, when you pray for something, believe that you have already received it. Then it will be yours."

Jesus was telling his disciples here that they could trust God for whatever they needed. He told them that when they pray, they should believe that God has already answered their prayer. That is called praying in faith. Faith is believing that God keeps his promises even when we can't see the answer yet.

So A.J. prayed and asked for the $10 that he needed for the game. When he prayed, he also thanked God for the game. He believed that God would really come through for him. Later that afternoon, A.J. received a phone call from a neighbor up the street. They wanted to hire A.J. to rake the leaves off their lawn. They offered A.J. $10 to do the job.

A.J. believed and received what he had prayed for! He was so excited, he wondered what else he could believe God for!

Join the Adventure!

Look up and read Mark 11:22-24 in your own Bible

PRAISE GOD

"Good girl, Posey!" Milo was training Posey to shake her paw. Posey was catching on quickly, so Milo gave Posey praise by telling her that she was a "good girl".

We praise our pets when they obey a command. Milo will draw a nice picture and her mom will praise her by telling her she is a good artist. We go to a concert or sports event and we praise the band or team for the great music or goal scored.

Praise is when we tell someone that we like and admire them or something they have done. We are showing them that we appreciate them. When you think about praise this way, then you realize that God deserves our praise! Read Psalm 146:2.

"I will praise the Lord all my life. I will sing praise to my God as long as I live."

God is so amazing and wonderful. He deserves our praise everyday. He made the universe and everything in it, including us. He loves us so much that he gave his Son, Jesus, to die for our sins. He has given us everything that we need to live a great life on earth, and he has given us the promise of heaven. That is why God is worth praising!

Take some time today to praise God. Say something like this – "God, you are so amazing! I love how you made the earth and all the animals. Your creation is so cool! You even made me, and you take care of me! You are awesome, God!"

Join the Adventure!

Look up and read all of Psalm 146 in your Bible

BAPTISM IS A SIGN OF FAITH

When I found out that my cousin was getting baptized at church, I had this picture in my mind of him perched on the dunk tank seat. The pastor would then use a ball to hit the target to release the seat to dunk my cousin in the water! It turns out, it doesn't happen quite like this.

The pastor asked my cousin if he believed in Jesus and what Jesus did for him on the cross. When he answered "yes", the pastor lowered him, head and all, under the water, and brought him back up again right away.

After the service I asked my cousin why he wanted to get baptized. He explained that the Bible says when we believe in Jesus we should get baptized. He wanted to obey God's Word. He told me to read Romans 6:4.

"By being baptized, we were buried with Christ into his death. Christ has been raised from the dead by the Father's glory. And like Christ we also can live a new life."

Baptism is a symbol of being buried with Jesus and raised to life again with him. When we choose to get baptized, we are telling Jesus and all those that are watching that we are serious about our faith in Jesus. It is like saying that we are leaving the old, sinful life behind in the water, and we are raised up to live a new faithful life with Jesus.

I want to obey God's Word. I am thinking I would like to get baptized. The dunk tank option sounds like fun, but I guess I could do it the way the church does!

Join the Adventure!

Read Acts 2:38 in your Bible

GOD IS OUR DEFENSE

The other day I was playing some street hockey with friends. In hockey the players that score the goals are called the forwards. The players that help protect the net are called the defense. If the forward tries to protect the net, they will never get a chance to score a goal themselves. It is the job of the defense to protect the net.

The Bible says in Psalm 3:3, **"Lord, you are like a shield that keeps me safe."** This is Jesus himself talking to his disciples.

Does loving our enemies mean that we just let them do bad things to us? No! God has promised to be our defense. Just like in hockey the defensive players protect the net, it is God's job to protect us!

We need to be concerned with doing the things that God has planned for us to do. If we are busy trying to get revenge on our enemies, we will never score any goals in life.

God's promise to you is that if you love your enemies that he will protect you and defend you. If someone has decided to cause trouble for you in your life, don't spend your energy trying to get revenge. Let God be your defense. Pray about your situation. Ask God to bless the person that is coming against you. Then be nice to them when you have opportunity. This is how you can love your enemies!

Join the Adventure!

Think of someone who has not been nice to you.
Now ask God to bless them

FEAR GO

Milo had almost fallen asleep when she heard a loud noise! Her heart started to beat faster and faster. She was afraid! Milo was so scared that she didn't even want to move. She pulled the covers up high to hide.

Then Milo remembered what the Bible says in Psalm 91:1

"Whoever rests in the shadow of the Most High God will be kept safe by the Mighty One." Milo could have stayed silent, frozen in fear, but instead she spoke this Bible verse out loud.

When you're laying there afraid, you need to say, "In the name of Jesus, fear go!" The name of Jesus is more powerful than any scary thing! Fear is no match for Jesus. The name of Jesus is more powerful than any problem that we have.

Milo lowered her blanket and told fear to leave in the name of Jesus. And it did! Then she fell asleep and had good dreams that night! The name of Jesus is powerful!

Join the Adventure!
Read 1 John 4:18 in your Bible

DE-CODE THIS BIBLE VERSE

Use the de-coder key on page 102 to discover what God has to say to you!

3: 20

THE MOST POWERFUL NAME

I used to get one great big cold that would last half the winter long. First my nose would get stuffy, then a cough would come on. It usually started by the end of November and would last until March! I would cough at night and it would keep me awake. It was awful!

Mom and Dad would give me medicine to help with the symptoms and of course pray for me! Things really started to change for me when I learned this Bible verse from Philippians 2:9.

"God lifted him [Jesus] up to the highest place. God gave him the name that is above every name."

This Bible verse shows how powerful the name of Jesus is! It says that at His name every knee shall bow. This means that our problems must listen to Jesus.

I realized that the name of Jesus was more powerful than a nagging cold. I started to pray for myself. I told the cold that it had to go because the name of Jesus was more powerful. I would pray something like this, "Cough go, in Jesus' name!" It was a simple prayer. I kept praying that everyday until the cough left!

I don't get colds like that anymore. They still come, but I just tell them to go in the name of Jesus, because the name of Jesus is more powerful!

Join the Adventure!

The next time you are not feeling well say this—Sickness "GO" in Jesus' name!

NEVER STOP

"This is the song that never ends
Yes, it goes on and on, my friend
Some people started singing it not knowing what it was
And they'll continue singing it forever just because
This is the song that never ends..."

Milo was singing "The Song that Never Ends" and it was driving A.J. crazy! On and on she just kept singing the same verse over and over again! A.J. asked his mom to make Milo stop, but she shrugged her shoulders and said Milo wasn't doing anything wrong.

How can anyone sing so long?! Here is another question. It says in the Bible in 1 Thessalonians 5:17 **"Never stop praying"**.

How can anyone pray all the time without stopping? If you prayed with your eyes closed, you would bump into things if you never stopped praying! But prayer isn't about closing our eyes, folding our hands and reciting certain words to God. Prayer is about knowing that God is always with you and being ready to communicate with Him at any time – with or without words.

Praying is saying thank you to God when you are happy about something. Or, when you are tempted to sin, ask God for help to do the right thing. It is asking God to help your friend see that Jesus is real. Praying is asking for the things you need when you need them. *Never stop praying* means you can pray anytime, anywhere for anything!

Join the Adventure!

Take a moment to pray to God right now

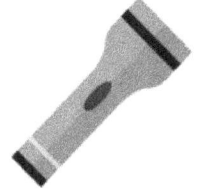

THANK GOD IN THE RAIN

Milo and A.J. felt very disappointed. The cousins were coming over to visit. They had big plans to play outside, but it was raining. All morning long Milo and A.J. moped around the house. Milo and A.J.'s mom finally said, "Surely there is something that you can be thankful for!" But they were only thinking about not being able to do what they wanted and could not see anything to be thankful for.

Their mom pulled a jar out of the kitchen cupboard. On the jar was written a Bible verse from Psalm 34:1. It read,

"I will thank the LORD at all times. My lips will always praise him."

The jar was filled with slips of paper with names and things written on them. Milo and A.J. had put the jar together last Thanksgiving holiday. Each slip of paper had something written on it that they could be thankful for. They could pull out a slip of paper and thank God for the person whose name was written there. Or they could thank God for things, like food, their house or toys. Milo and A.J. pulled out several of the pieces of paper and read what was written on them.

Even though it was raining, there were many things that they could be thankful for! They took a moment to pray and thank God for some of the things on the slips of paper. After that, Milo and A.J. didn't feel disappointed anymore! Then they wrote a list of indoor activities that they could so when their cousins were over. There is always something to be thankful for!

Join the Adventure!

Make your own thankfulness jar! Write as many things as you can think of on slips of paper. Read them and say thanks to God for his goodness!

GIVE THANKS TO GOD

It was bedtime and Milo's mom encouraged her to think of two things to thank God for that day. So, Milo prayed.

"Thank you, God, for the food I ate today, thank you for school, thank you for Mrs. Garba my teacher, thank for my friends Ronan, Sierra and Hayley, thank you for Posey, Mom, Dad and A.J., thank you for my toys, thank you for gymnastics, thank you for Grandma and Grandpa and all my cousins, thank you for my house, and thank you for the birds outside my window that chirp, and most of all thank you for Jesus. In Jesus Name, Amen!"

Wow! Milo's mom was surprised by the long list. She had only suggested that Milo think of two things, but Milo had many more things to thank God for. The Bible says in Ephesians 5:20,

"Always give thanks to God the Father for everything. Give thanks to him in the name of our Lord Jesus Christ."

Milo was doing what the Bible says to do, she was giving thanks to God for everything! God is so good to us. There are many things everyday that we should thank him for.

Join the Adventure!

Take some time now to think of at least two things to say "thank you" to God for.

PRAY FOR OTHERS

Milo's plans to play with her friend, Ronan, were canceled because Ronan was not feeling well. He had a cough and a fever. Milo felt bad for Ronan. She wanted to help but didn't know what she could do.

Milo's dad read a Bible verse from 1 Timothy 2:1.

"First, I want you to pray for all people. Ask God to help and bless them."

"Do you remember what we did the last time you were not feeling well, Milo?" Dad asked.

"Well, I laid on the couch and rested. Oh, ya. Now I remember. The first thing we did was pray that God would heal me!" Milo was excited. Now she knew how she could help her friend Ronan. She could pray for him!

So Milo, with a little help from her dad, prayed for Ronan.

"Dear God, please help Ronan to feel better. Thank you that he has been healed by the wounds of Jesus. Oh, and God, help us to be able to play together soon! In Jesus' Name, Amen!"

God wants us to pray for other people. When we hear that a friend, family member or neighbor needs help, the first thing we should do is pray for them. We can even pray when they don't need help. We can ask God to "bless them", just like the Bible verse says.

Milo planned to call Ronan tomorrow to reschedule their play-date. Milo was confident that God heard her prayer!

Join the Adventure!

Think of someone that you can pray for right now

THE CHURCH IS GOD'S PLAN

People are always "making plans". They plan what they are going to wear to school the next day. They plan to get together with a friend after school. They plan what they are going to do on the weekend.

I know of an awesome plan! But it's not the kind of plan I've been talking about here. This plan is God's plan for *all* people. It says in the Bible in Ephesians 3:10, 11 (NLT), **"God's purpose was to use the church to display his wisdom in its rich variety...this was his eternal plan."**

Before even the world was created it was God's plan that all people be a part of the church, which is the family of people who believe in Jesus. God wants to do so many things in our lives and in this world, but his *plan* is to use the church to do it.

Let me give you an example. I heard a story about a boy named Landon. He lives in the U.S. He had a friend named Rick. A lot of parents didn't like their kids hanging out with Rick because he did bad things sometimes. Landon, however, brought his friend Rick to church with him every week. One day Rick got saved! He became a Christian! He kept coming to church and then one day his mom came too, and she got saved! See God's plan was to reach more people for Jesus through the church. That is why the church is God's Plan!

Join the Adventure!

Make a plan to go to church this week

DE-CODE THIS BIBLE VERSE

Use the de-coder key on page 102 to discover what God has to say to you!

4: 29

Read the rest of this verse in your Bible!

PRAY FOR YOURSELF

Milo brought a note home from school. Apparently, she had a long overdue book from the library. The notice said that she would have to pay $25 if she did not return "Wild Cats" by the end of the month. Milo frantically searched through her bedroom. Maybe the book got put away on the shelf with all her other books. Or maybe it was accidently kicked under the bed. Or maybe it was under a pile of stuffies.

"Mom!" Milo called, "I can't find the book! What am I going to do?" Milo was worried. She didn't have $25 to pay for the book.

Milo's mom had Milo sit down and take a breath. Milo was worrying when she should have been praying. Together, they read this Bible verse from Philippians 4:6.

"Don't worry about anything. No matter what happens, tell God about everything. Ask and pray, and give thanks to him."

Our problems matter to God. He tells us in the Bible not to worry about things, but to tell him about them. Milo and her mom prayed that God would help them find the book. Milo thanked God that he would have the solution to her problem.

A thought had occurred to Milo. She had not yet looked behind the big pillow in her reading corner. Sometimes she would save a book there when she was planning on going back to it later. Sure enough "Wild Cats" was there, safe and sound behind the pillow!

When Milo stopped worrying and prayed to God about her need, the answer came! It doesn't matter what our need is, the Bible tells us that we should pray about everything!

Join the Adventure!

Think of a need that you have. Ask God to help you with it

MAKE GOING TO CHURCH YOUR HABIT

Milo loves to work in the garden with her mom in spring. In order for a plant to grow, it needs some vital things. Vital means necessary for life! Life doesn't happen without these things. Plants need sunlight, water and soil with certain nutrients.

There are some vital things that *we* need to grow physically like food and proper sleep, but did you know that there are vital things we need to grow spiritually as well? To grow spiritually we need to learn from the Bible, we need to pray, and worship God and we need to have relationships with other Christians. This is how we grow. These vital things are only found when we are connected to the church.

Sure, you can read the Bible on your own, but God has given us pastors and teachers to help us understand His Word. Relationships with other Christians are important because they can help us when we are having a hard time doing what is right. Hebrews 10:25 says, **"And let us not give up meeting together. Some are in the habit of doing this. Instead, let us encourage one another with words of hope."**

We need to be connected to the Church. We can only grow and be all that God has created us for when we are connected to His Church because the church is God's Plan!

Join the Adventure!

Look up Colossians 1:18 in your Bible

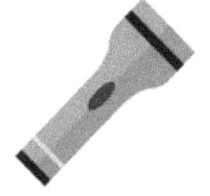

YOU WILL RECEIVE POWER

I was watching a video of powerful explosions. I could almost feel the ground shake. It was awesome! It got me thinking about some other things that are powerful. What about a body builder? They sure have a lot of power in their muscles! A monster truck is powerful. Have you ever seen one up close? Or heard that engine roar? That is power! It would be cool to have that kind of power. The truth is, we have a better power!

Read Acts 1:8 - **"But you will receive power when the Holy Spirit comes on you."**

When we put our faith in what Jesus has done for us, his Spirit comes to live inside of us. No one has greater power than God! God stretched out the sky and set the ground in place. He created billions of stars each one larger than our entire planet and named every one of them. He is so wise and strong that we can't even imagine it. It is crazy to think that this same power lives in us, but it is true!

When we face challenges in life like being sick, learning something hard at school or trying to get along with someone who bugs us, we have the power of God in us to help us overcome! That is a better power than anything this earth has to offer us!

Join the Adventure!

Look up Ephesians 3:20 in your Bible

BE BRAVE

Each year in the last month of school all the classes in the school get to take turns swimming at the community pool. My friends and I were taking turns walking off the pool deck into the water. We were trying to see how far we got before we sank. We were trying to walk on water like Jesus and Peter did in the Bible!

Matthew 14 tells the story of when the disciples were in a boat on the Sea of Galilee. Jesus walked out to them on the water! At first they were afraid.

"Right away Jesus called out to them, 'Be brave! It is I. Don't be afraid.'" (Matthew 14:27)

Then, Peter said if it is you Jesus, call me out to walk on the water. And that is what Peter did! For a few moments Peter was walking on water! But then he began to sink and Jesus had to save him.

I find it interesting that Peter started to look at the wind and the waves and then he got afraid and began to sink. He should have been looking at the fact that he was walking on water! His focus was all wrong!

Sometimes we have scary things that we need to do in life. Like go somewhere we've never gone before like camp or a new school. We should remember the words of Jesus! "Be brave! It is I. Don't be afraid."

God is always with us to help us walk on water, figuratively speaking! As for me and my friends, we all sunk as soon as we stepped out on the pool water. But we had fun trying!

Join the Adventure!

Read Matthew 14:22-33 in your Bible

GOD WILL GO WITH YOU

This year is my last year in this school. I have been at this school since kindergarten. Next year I will go to a different school in town for Grade 6. I gotta admit, I'm feeling a bit nervous. It's been a good run here. I know all the teachers, I know where all the hallways lead and we are the oldest kids in the school. Next year we are going to be the youngest! There will be a lot of kids there I don't know too. How will I find everything? It's a bigger school with more grades.

SATTAR gave me this Bible verse from Deuteronomy 31:6 to help me feel better.

"The Lord your God will go with you. He will never leave you. He will never desert you."

He explained that Moses told this to the Israelites when they moved into a new land. The Israelites had been slaves in Egypt for many years. Then God used Moses to save them from slavery and bring them into a new land that would be their home. They were afraid. Even though slavery was bad, there were many new and scary challenges to face in the new land. Moses encouraged them that God would be with them every step of the way.

It sure makes me feel better when I think that God is with me wherever I go! Especially, when it is some where I have never been before. Whether you are going across the street to play at a friend's house, or going to a whole new school like me, God is with you!

Join the Adventure!

Read Ephesians 6:10 in your Bible

GROW THE CHURCH

Milo had a friend at school that she wanted to bring to church. She asked her Sunday School teacher at church to call her friend to invite them to church. Milo thought that it was up to the teacher to do the inviting. God has called us, the church, to work with Him to grow the church. It is our job as part of the church to tell our family, friends and neighbours about Jesus. It is up to Milo to invite her friend!

In the early days of the church, no one thought that it was only the pastor's job to tell people about Jesus. They all worked together. Read Acts 2:42-43.

"The believers studied what the apostles taught. They shared their lives together. They ate and prayed together. Everyone was amazed at what God was doing."

Because they all worked together, God did many miracles through them and many, many people came to know the truth about Jesus. In fact, the news about Jesus started to spread throughout the world. Now there are believers in Jesus all over the world!

Continued on next page

This reminds me of the story of a boy in India named Raahi. He learned about Jesus from some pastors in town and began praying for his mom to be healed because she was really sick. He kept praying and after a few months she got healed and Raahi's whole family became Christians! God used Raahi, not the pastors, to reach his family for Jesus, and he wants to use you to reach your family and friends and neighbours. The Church is God's Plan!

Join the Adventure!

Read Acts 2:14-41 in your Bible

DE-CODE THIS BIBLE VERSE

Use the de-coder key on page 102 to discover what God has to say to you!

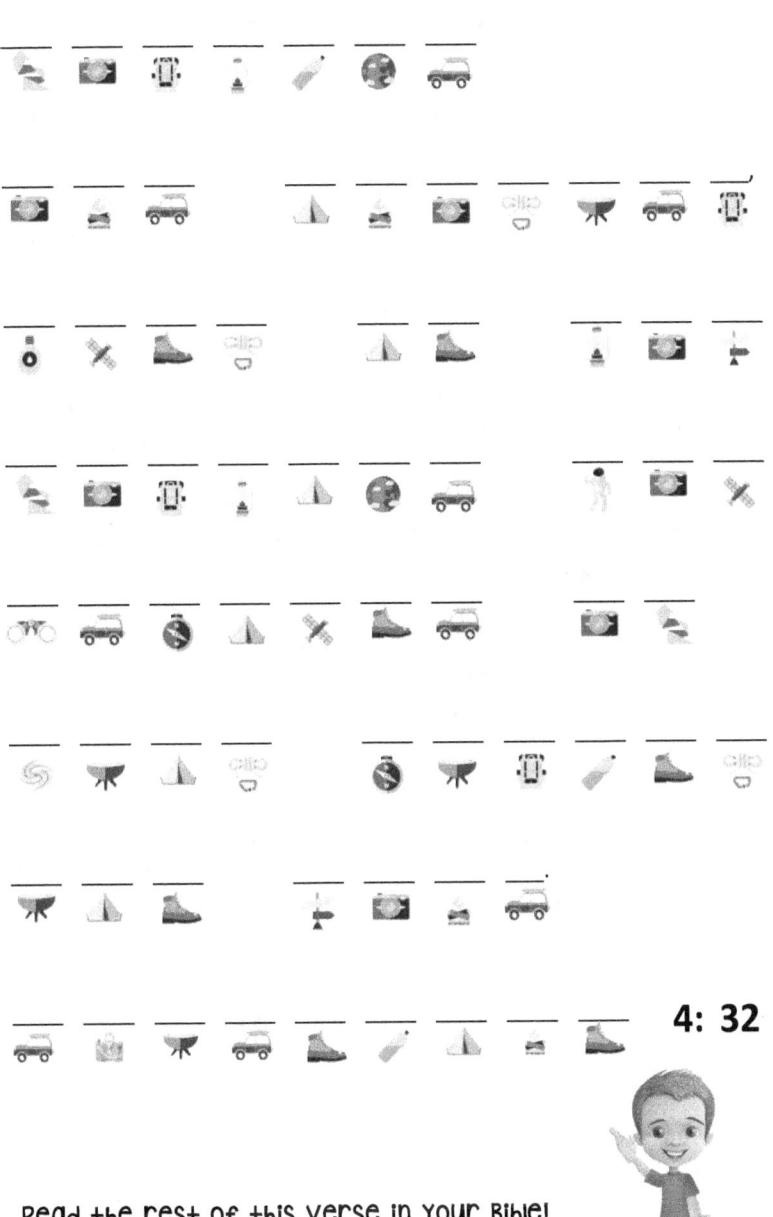

4: 32

Read the rest of this verse in your Bible!

LOVE YOUR ENEMIES

It was family movie night at Milo's house! They were watching an intergalactic space battle movie. Milo loves movies about outer-space!

When you go to see a movies like this, there is a hero and a villain. In these movies, the villain does nasty stuff and the hero tries to capture the villain. Everyone naturally cheers for the hero to win and wants the villain to die. This is what movies are all about. It is fun to watch movies like this.

But when you think about it, this is opposite to what God wants. The world says, "hate your enemies". The Bible says we should love our enemies, not hate them.

Read Matthew 5:44 – **"But here is what I tell you. Love your enemies."**

This was Jesus himself teaching his friends! God wants to give people who do bad things a chance to turn away from their sin. The only way they will do that is if someone shows them God's love.

We need to start thinking differently about our enemies. Instead of hating them when they do bad stuff, we need to love them. We need to pray for them, be kind to them, do nice things for them. Only then will they begin to change. Love your enemies.

Join the Adventure!

Read 1 Timothy 2:1 in your Bible

HOLY SPIRIT GROWS GOOD FRUIT

My favorite fruit is the peach. I love when they are in season. When I bite into one and the juice runs down my chin and onto my neck, I know I have found a good peach! Sweet and juicy – that is what makes them so good.

Did you know that God is a fruit farmer? It says so in the Bible! Read Galatians 5:22 for yourself if you don't believe me.

"But the fruit the Holy Spirit produces is love, joy and peace. It is being patient, kind and good. It is being faithful and gentle and having control of oneself."

When we put our faith in Jesus, God's Spirit comes to live in our hearts. One of the reasons he comes to live in us is so he can grow good fruit in our lives! The Bible uses fruit to describe the good things that God wants to do in our hearts. He wants to help us to love others and to be patient and kind. He wants us to have joy and faith. He wants us to have self-control.

God's Spirit, who lives in us, helps to grow this fruit in our lives because he knows they are good. If we allow this fruit to grow in our lives, we will have a good life! What is your favorite fruit? Next time you take a bite out of your favorite fruit, think about the fruit that the Holy Spirit wants to grow in your life.

Join the Adventure!

Pray and ask God to help you grow good fruit in your life

GOD'S WORD IS LIKE A SEED

Each spring Mom lets me plant sweet corn in the garden. It takes a few days for the corn seed to germinate and poke through the surface of the soil. Then it takes even longer before we can harvest that yummy corn. I am usually pretty impatient about the whole process. I wish I could just plant the seed and have corn on the cob the next day! But it doesn't work that way.

The Bible calls itself a seed. Read Mark 4:14.

"The seed the farmer plants is God's message."

God's Word or message is like a seed. I think the Bible calls itself a seed for a few reasons. One of the reasons that I think is because it takes time for a seed to produce the plant that we want. In my case corn. But as long as we take care of the seed we planted, by watering and weeding, it will produce the harvest we are expecting!

God's Word is like that. It is never a waste when we tell people about Jesus. Telling people about Jesus is like planting the seed of God's Word in their lives. Sometimes we feel like there was no point to telling a friend about Jesus because they haven't put their faith in him. But the seed of God's Word is alive! It just sometimes takes time to grow in someone's life. It is important to keep watering and weeding that seed by showing our friend God's love and praying for them too.

Join the Adventure!

Think of a friend that you can tell about Jesus

GOD'S POWER IN YOU

Milo had a lion stuffie sitting on her bed. She would play with it and pretend that it was a real, powerful lion. Lions are the king of the jungle. They are very powerful. Milo also had a cute little pink poodle stuffie on her bed. Milo has a lot of stuffies! Toy poodles are one of the smallest dogs around. They're cute and cuddly but really don't make the best guard dogs!

It would look really silly if a huge lion thought it was a poodle! Milo could just put a leash on it, and tie pretty bows in its hair! If the lion really knew who he was, he wouldn't put up with all of that!

Once you ask Jesus, God's Son, into your heart, you are like the lion. God puts His power inside of you! Read Romans 8:11.

"The Spirit of the God who raised Jesus from the dead is living in you."

God has created you to do amazing things for Him. God's given you the power to do things with Him that you could never do without him.

You're not like the little poodle, you're like the lion. When you are facing a challenge like learning a math problem or dealing with someone who is not being nice to you, you have God's power in you to help because God's Spirit lives in you!

Join the Adventure!

Read 2 Peter 1:3 in your Bible

GOD WANTS EVERYONE TO BE A PART OF THE CHURCH

There are people in every one of our lives that don't like us for whatever reason and don't treat us very good. These people could be considered our enemies. We often want to treat these people the same way they treat us. If they tell lies about us behind our backs, we want to gossip about them. Or if they hit us, we want to hit back.

But the Bible tells us in 1 Timothy 2:4 **"He wants all people to be saved. He wants them to come to know the truth."**

But how do we share the love of Jesus with people who are not nice to us? Romans 12:20 says "If your enemies are hungry, feed them". This doesn't mean walking around with groceries so we can feed our enemies. "Here Joe, have a loaf of bread". That would be silly!

This Bible verse means that if we see that our enemy has a need, we should try to help them. Maybe your enemy is at school and they don't have a pen for class. You could lend them one. Or maybe they forgot their lunch that day. You could share yours. Or even better - buy them a chocolate bar! Take the first step in making peace with them. To feed your enemies is to be *kind* to them. Use kind words, pray for them.

When we do this people will see that God is real and that he cares for them! This is important because God wants everyone to be a part of the church!

Join the Adventure!

Think of someone that you can be kind to today

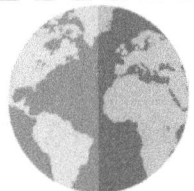

A CHILD OF GOD IS WHO YOU ARE

Milo's dad had used a website on the computer to learn more about his family history. He knew about his parents, grand parents and great-grand parents, but he didn't know much about the family that came before his great-grand parents.

When he did his research, he found out that way back in the family line, one of his great-great-great-great-great uncles had been a thief! A.J. had thought that was exciting, but the news upset Milo. She didn't like the thought that she had family that had been in prison.

Milo's dad encouraged her that the family history wasn't as important as knowing whose child we are now! He read John 1:12 and 13 to Milo.

"Some people did accept him [Jesus] and did believe in his name. He gave them the right to become children of God. To be a child of God has nothing to do with human parents. Children of God are not born because of human choice or because a husband wants them to be born. They are born because of what God does."

When we put our faith in Jesus, we become children of God! It doesn't matter who is in our family line or what they may have done. We are forgiven, made right with God and become his child when we believe in Jesus! When Milo heard that, she wanted to know if there were more Christians in her family line. So her dad continued his research!

Join the Adventure!

Read Romans 8:16 in your Bible

DE-CODE THIS BIBLE VERSE

Use the de-coder key on page 102 to discover what God has to say to you!

119:11

DREAM BIG

Mom and Dad told me and Milo that we were going to take the camper out for a couple of weeks this summer. I was excited when I heard that. I love camping. We live pretty close to a park with great camping spots and an awesome lake with a sandy beach. I imagined playing in the waves and building lots of sand castles for two weeks.

Then Mom and Dad told us where we were going with the camper. We were taking it to the mountains and to the dinosaur park! Now I was really excited! This trip was shaping up to be more than I could have imagined! My parents are so cool for planning a trip like this.

God is like this too! It says so in Ephesians 3:20.

"God is able to do far more than we could ever ask or imagine. He does everything by his power that is working in us."

Whatever we can dream up for our lives, God's plans for us are more awesome than we could ever ask or imagine! God wants us to have great lives. Lives with a great purpose – to share the truth about Jesus with the world!

We should have big dreams and big plans for our lives. Just know that when you are dreaming – God can do more than we could ever ask or imagine!

Join the Adventure!

Write down a "dream" that you have.
Now talk to God about it

BE GRATEFUL WE ARE FREE

Milo's class was taking a trip on the school bus to visit the Pioneer Museum in another town. At the museum they saw how families had come from another country across the ocean leaving many family members behind and most of their possessions to come to a new country with the hope of starting a better life for their family. The people had to work very hard to start a new life in a country where they did not speak the language. They had to cut wood from the forests to build their homes and use horses to plow the ground to plant crops to have food for the very cold winter months.

The children in these families also had to work very hard. Milo asked one of the museum interpreters why these people would have left a comfortable life in a country they knew to come and work so hard to start a new life. The interpreter read this verse from Galatians 5:1

"Christ has set us free to enjoy our freedom."

He explained to Milo's class that the country where they came from did not allow the people to read the Bible for themselves. The leaders of those countries were very controlling and did not want the people to have freedom. They decided to sail over seas and start a new life so they could freely teach their children about Jesus.

The interpreter encouraged the kids to be grateful that these pioneers had made the sacrifice to come and build a new life in a foreign country. It was because of this, that it is possible for the kids to go on school field trips and enjoy so many other freedoms that we have in this country!

Join the Adventure!

Read Acts 13:39 in your Bible

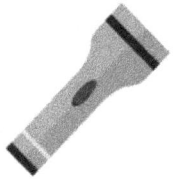

WISDOM WILL KEEP YOU SAFE

The other day when we went on our field trip, I had forgotten to bring my water bottle. We had gone to Grand Prix Amusements. There were go carts, bumper cars, bumper boats, batting cages and more. It was so hot that day and I was so thirsty! How could I have forgotten something so important? Water is necessary to live! Especially on such a hot day.

Proverbs 4:5 and 6 encourages us not to forget something else that is important!

"Get wisdom, and get understanding. Don't forget my words or turn away from them. Stay close to wisdom, and she will keep you safe."

Proverbs tells us that we should not forget God's Words! We get wisdom and understanding by reading the Bible. In fact, the Bible is the best place to get wisdom and understanding. And having wisdom keeps us safe. Just like drinking water on a hot day keeps us safe and healthy.

That is why it is so important that we don't forget to read the Bible! When we are on summer holidays, our routines change, or fly out the window altogether! Every day is different from the next. My plan this summer is to get up early enough to make sure I have time in the morning to read the Bible before I go about my busy day because I don't want to forget!

Join the Adventure!

Make a plan to read your Bible everyday

JESUS LOVED TO TELL STORIES

Did you know that Jesus was a great story-teller? The New Testament has over 30 different stories recorded that Jesus told. We call these stories, parables. Jesus told parables to teach people the truth about God. After all, who doesn't love a story? One day crowds of people had gathered around Jesus on the shores of Galilee to hear what he had to say. Jesus began to teach them many things about God by telling them parables.

"The kingdom of heaven is like a treasure that was hidden in a field. When a man found it, he hid it again. He was very happy. So he went and sold everything he had. And he bought that field."
Matthew 13:44

In this parable, Jesus taught the people that God's kingdom was very valuable. He said it was like a hidden treasure. The man in the story sold everything he had just so he could get that treasure. He knew that treasure was worth more than anything else he had.

Jesus was telling the people that they should feel the same way about God's kingdom. It should be worth more to us than anything else in our life! For example, in God's kingdom, there is forgiveness. If we want God's kingdom in our life, then we need to give up unforgiveness! Or, in God's kingdom there is love. If we want God's kingdom in our life, we should work at loving others like God does!

Join the Adventure!

Read Matthew 13:45-46 in your Bible

WE ARE RESPONSIBLE FOR OURSELVES

Milo and her friend, Ronan, went to the local swimming pool to swim one afternoon. The pool had a rule that in order to swim in the deep end without a life jacket, a person would have to swim four widths of the pool. Ronan swam the widths right away and was allowed to go in the deep end without his life jacket.

Milo didn't think that she could do the laps. She sat on the side of the swimming pool and sulked. "It's not fair," she told her mom. "I should be allowed to go in the deep end without doing laps because my friend is there." Milo's mom reminded her of what the Bible says in Galatians 6:4-5.

"Pay careful attention to your own work, for then you will get the satisfaction of a job well done, and you won't need to compare yourself to anyone else. For we are each responsible for our own conduct."

She explained to Milo that just because something is "hard" to do doesn't mean that you can't do it. She knew that Milo could swim the laps on her own. It was important that Milo do it for herself too for her safety.

Just like Milo was responsible to do her own laps, we are responsible in life to learn how to do things for ourselves. As we grow, we learn how to clean our own room, make our own friendships and eventually live on our own. It is important when we are young to be responsible for the small things so we can be ready to be responsible for the big things later.

Join the Adventure!

Read Luke 16:10 in your Bible

WE NEED FRIENDS

Today my friend Joely and I built a go-kart out of scrap materials Dad had in the garage. I'm glad that Joely was with me to help. I couldn't have done it without her! She helped hold the boards in place while I screwed them together. We used wheels from a couple of old lawnmowers. She helped me lift the go-kart up while I installed the wheels. Then she painted cool flames on it. She is good at that kind of thing! The Bible has a lot to say about friends. For starters, it says that two people are better than one. Read for yourself in Ecclesiastes 4:9-10.

"Two people are better than one. They can help each other in everything they do. Suppose either of them falls down. Then the one can help the other one up. But suppose a person falls down and doesn't have anyone to help them up. Then feel sorry for that person!"

In the book of Genesis, God said that it was not good for Adam to be alone, so he created Eve for Adam. Life has many challenges. Our friends can help us during the hard times.

They also make the good times much more fun! Our go-kart didn't have a motor, so Joely and I had to take turns pushing it with a broomstick. I couldn't have done that by myself!

Join the Adventure!

Read John 15:14 in your Bible

DE-CODE THIS BIBLE VERSE

Use the de-coder key on page 102 to discover what God has to say to you!

Read the rest of this verse in your Bible!

LOOK AT YOURSELF FIRST

I couldn't believe it! I was three pieces away from finishing my model of a dinosaur skeleton and I was missing the third last piece. Or was I?

I ranted and complained about the company that packaged and sold that model. How could they be so sloppy in their work? Then SATTAR reminded me about the time I had the same issue with one of my building block sets. I got stuck at a step and couldn't go any further until I had the missing piece. I blamed the company that time too for not putting it in the package. Then...I found the missing piece. I had dropped it on the floor, and it got kicked under the couch.

SATTAR suggested that this might be a similar situation to the building block incident. He suggested that I was a little too quick to blame others for my own problem. He read these Bible verses from Matthew 7:3-5

"You look at the bit of sawdust in your friend's eye. But you pay no attention to the piece of wood in your own eye. How can you say to your friend, 'Let me take the bit of sawdust out of your eye'? How can you say this while there is a piece of wood in your own eye? You pretender! First take the piece of wood out of your own eye. Then you will be able to see clearly to take the bit of sawdust out of your friend's eye."

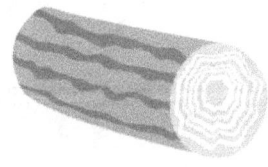

I am like the person in the story who has a piece of wood in their eye. I wanted to blame others when I was the one who had the problem. The truth is, no one is perfect! Except for Jesus of course! We will always meet people that have problems or encounter situations that are frustrating. We should not be too quick to judge others or blame situations. We need to take responsibility for our part - you know, the piece of wood in our eye!

I'm glad these Bible verses aren't talking about a real piece of wood. That would be painful! Once I got the wood out of my eye, so to speak, I started to look for the missing piece of my model. And...I found it! This time it had been pushed under the area rug. I got to finish my model and learn a valuable lesson!

Join the Adventure!

Read Matthew 7:1-2 in your Bible

WE ARE IN TRAINING

I decided that I wanted to run in a local 3-mile race. I think I was having a moment of temporary insanity when I signed up! I started training and quickly realized that 3 miles is a long distance! I wanted to quit. The training was hard.

SATTAR encouraged me not to quit. He assured me that I would feel good about myself if I finished the race. I would be stronger and faster too!

Just like I didn't like training for this race, I don't always like it when I get disciplined by my parents. Or, I don't like it when I am facing a hard test at school. The Bible has a verse for these kinds of situations! It is found in Hebrews 12:7.

"Put up with hard times. God uses them to train you. He is treating you as his children. What children are not trained by their parents?"

My body is getting stronger from my race training. When I face hard times with the attitude that I can grow from the situation I will get stronger on the inside! I gain the skills I need to face even tougher situations. Sometimes life can be hard. But with God's help we can be strong and have a good life!

I ran the race on the weekend. I came in 6th place out of 15 in my age category. Not bad! I might keep training to see if I can do better in my next race!

Join the Adventure!

Read 1 Corinthians 9:24-27 in your Bible

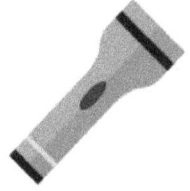

GOD'S BUILDING BLOCKS

One day I was trying to teach Posey some basic commands and tricks. "Posey, come!" I would say. And Posey would stay. "Posey, sit!" I would say. And Posey would stand. "Posey, shake paw!" And Posey would roll over. Yeesh! I couldn't even get my dog to do what I wanted when I spoke. It boggles my mind to think that when God spoke in the beginning, that he created the universe!

The Bible says in Genesis 1:3 Then God said, **"Let there be light,"** and there was light. God just spoke. Bada boom, bada bing! "Light be!" And light was! Read the whole chapter of Genesis 1 and you will see that God spoke to create everything we see in outer space and our natural world including people! He had an idea of what he wanted to create, then he spoke and it was created. Wow! God is so creative and powerful!

Join the Adventure!

Read the first chapter of Genesis

CHOOSE FRIENDS WISELY

The other day I was hanging out with a few of the kids from my class at school. We went over to one of their houses. It was hot outside, so we decided to go inside and watch a movie. My friend was scrolling through the selections when he stopped at a scary movie. It was an 'R' rated movie, the kind that I know I am not allowed to watch. A bunch of the kids said to pick that movie. I spoke up and said I didn't want to watch that one. But they took a vote and decided to watch it anyway. I decided to go home. My friend Joely came with me. She knew that it wasn't right to watch a movie like that. Those kinds of movies just put fear inside you. Who wants that?

I am glad that Joely came with me. She is a good friend. The Bible talks about choosing good friends in Proverbs 13:20.

"Walk with wise people and become wise. A companion of foolish people suffers harm."

If we hang out with people who know right from wrong, we will be wise. When we hang out with people who do not know right from wrong it will lead to trouble. I think my other friends are going to find that out tonight when they have bad dreams from watching that movie. I'm glad I have a wise friend like Joely. We went back to my house and had milkshakes and read jokes from my favorite joke book!

Join the Adventure!

Read Proverbs 12:26 in your Bible

WHAT DOES THE BIBLE SAY

SATTAR had drawn a maze for Milo to do. Milo loved doing mazes. There was usually a character at one end that had to find some kind of treasure at the other end. On this maze, SATTAR had forgotten to put the starting spot. Milo did not know where to start the maze.

Life can be like a maze. There are a lot of decisions to make every day. It is a good thing that God has shown us where the starting point is in life! Read Proverbs 1:7.

"If you really want to gain knowledge, you must begin by having respect for the Lord."

Respecting God is the starting point to get the knowledge we need to make good choices in life. To respect God means to look to him and to his Word for the right way to live. When we choose to do things God's way, we are respecting him. When we obey our parents, we are respecting God because it says to obey in the Bible. When we tell the truth, we are respecting God because the Bible tells us to be honest. When we respect God, we will gain the knowledge we need to live a good life!

Milo told SATTAR that he forgot to put a starting point on the maze so he added one so she could finish the maze!

Join the Adventure!

Read 1 Peter 5:6 in your Bible

Maze

PLANT A GOOD CROP

It is a super hot day today. Dad wanted me to mow the lawn today. I figured I would do it first thing in the morning before it got really hot. Dad said because I got the lawn mowed right away (and I did a good job) that I could go to a movie in the afternoon with my friends. Awesome! Air-conditioning here I come!

I like when I obey my parents. Good things happen. The Bible verse Galatians 6:7 talks about this.

"A man gathers a crop from what he plants."

When a farmer plants corn seed he will harvest corn. This Bible verse is telling us that if we want good things to happen in our life, we need to plant good things! Obeying our parents is a good thing to do. I can only imagine what would have happened if I had disobeyed Dad and not mown the lawn. I probably would have been grounded and been given more chores to do!

If we harvest what we plant, when we plant bad things we will harvest bad things. If we disobey our parents, we will harvest some kind of punishment. I like harvesting good things. I'm going to keep this Bible verse in mind the next time I am tempted to disobey!

Join the Adventure!

Read Galatians 6:7-9 in your Bible

DE-CODE THIS BIBLE VERSE

Use the de-coder key on page 102 to discover what God has to say to you!

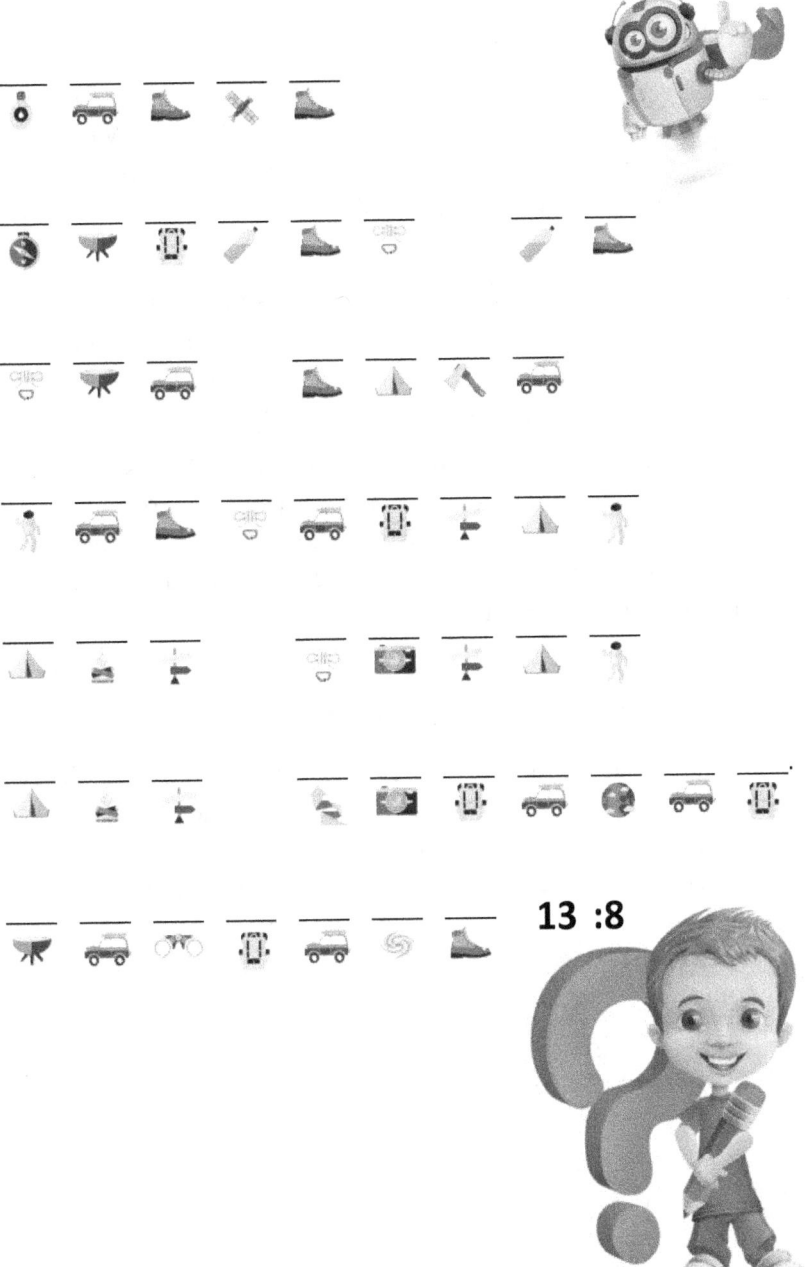

13 :8

IT IS BEST TO TRUST GOD

We had a game day in gym class today. We got to play a bunch of fun games like Duck Duck Goose, Tag and Tug of War. Tug of War was my favorite. That is where two teams would each grab the end of a rope and pull until one team is pulled across a dividing line.

Before we started, I looked at the rope, and I looked at the opposing team, and I did not trust that the rope was going to hold. It looked like a thin rope. I did not have confidence that the rope was not going to break.

I told my teacher that I didn't trust the rope. He assured me that the rope was dependable. I was a bit worried. I didn't trust the rope, but I did trust my gym teacher! He had experience with the rope, and he was always concerned about our safety. I figured I could trust him.

Psalm 118:8 says, **"It is better to go to the Lord for safety than to trust in mere human beings."**

Sometimes God asks us to do something and we don't understand why. Sometimes he asks us to be nice to someone who isn't nice to us for example. We can't understand why, but we can trust God that he is asking us to do it for a good reason. We can have confidence that he has our best in mind. I guess you can say that trust is the same thing as having confidence in someone.

Well, my trust in my gym teacher paid off. The rope didn't break, and my team won the Tug of War!

Join the Adventure!

Read Psalm 20:7 in your Bible

FRIENDS MAKE US BETTER

I like to collect pocket-knives. Milo just recently gave me a wood handled pocket-knife with my name engraved on it. I love it! For a knife to work properly it needs to be sharp. You can't cut a rope or whittle the end of a stick with a dull knife. I have a knife sharpener. It is a stick made out of special steel meant for sharpening knives. You run the knife blade over the steel at an angle and it makes the knife sharp again. There is a Bible verse about sharpening knives, well, sort of! Read Proverbs 27:17.

"As iron sharpens iron, so one person sharpens another."

This Bible verse found in Proverbs is saying that you can rub an iron edge on iron, and it will make the iron edge sharp. The iron edge is made better. In the same way, one person sharpens another. This means that our friends can make us better.

Sometimes, we can have disagreements with our friends. When we work the problem out with our friends, we become better. We learn how to speak the truth to each other, how to really listen and how to forgive each other. We get to practice loving people with our friends. God wants us to grow and become more like him every day. Our friends help us do that!

Join the Adventure!

Read Proverbs 16:18 in your Bible

GOD HAS A GREAT IMAGINATION

A.J. and Milo were bored so SATTAR challenged them to a nature scavenger hunt. He told them to go and find as many different kinds of leaves as they possibly could. They took a sand pail out of the sandbox and started their hunt in their own yard and then moved up the street. Posey came along to keep them company. After a short distance they had already filled up their pail with 34 different types of leaves! They had to squish them down to make them fit in the pail. There were long and skinny leaves. Short and fat leaves. Teeny-tiny leaves. Leaves bigger than the palm of A.J.'s hand. There was ten different shades of green, leaves with yellow stripes, and others with red and orange speckles throughout. Some were smooth, some were rough. Genesis 1:11 tells us that God created the plants.

"Then God said, 'Let the land produce plants.'"

Wow! God sure is creative! The idea for all these different kinds of plants came from the mind of God! He also created all the animals, birds, fish and lizards. God is so awesome!

Join the Adventure!

Go on a scavenger hunt in your neighborhood and see how many different kinds of leaves you can find

THE BIBLE IS YOUR INSTRUCTION BOOK FOR LIFE

When I first got SATTAR he came to me in a box. That's right, I assembled him myself! With some help from Dad of course. SATTAR is a very complex robot and it took me months to put him together. But it was worth it. He is so much fun to have around now!

I had a really slow start. The company I ordered him from had forgotten to put the assembly instructions in the box with all the parts. I tried to assemble him on my own without the manual but it was impossible! There were so many parts that I just didn't know what to do with. Finally, I called the company and had them send me the assembly instruction manual.

Life is like that. It can be complex. I may be young now, but I know that decisions get harder to make as you get older too. The good news is that there is help available. The Bible is an instruction manual for life. It says so itself in Psalm 119:105.

"Your word is like a lamp that shows me the way. It is like a light that guides me."

The Bible has so many instructions on the best way to live. It helps us make good decisions that lead to a great life and helps us deal with challenges when they come. Just like a good instruction manual.

Join the Adventure!

Read Hebrews 4:12 in your Bible

THE PATH OF LIFE

Milo loves gymnastics. Each week on Saturday she goes to a gymnastics class where she learns how to do cartwheels, forward rolls and walk on the balance beam. The balance beam is a very narrow beam. In order to stay on the beam, Milo looks forward, points her toes and uses her arms to balance. It can be tricky to stay on the balance beam because it is so narrow!

The Bible says in Psalm 16:11, **"You always show me the path of life."** God is telling us in this Bible verse that he shows us the best way to live. The way to have a great life is narrow, or simple like a balance beam. We should learn about how to live right and do God's will by reading the Bible. It has everything we need to know on how to live right.

For example, God's path of life says we should be happy for people when things go right for them. The world's way is to feel jealous. Jealousy leads to destruction. Jealousy can ruin a good friendship. God's way is better. You can have peace trusting that God has good things for you too.

The next time you balance on a curb, or walk on the balance beam at school, think about this Bible verse and how you can do things God's way!

Join the adventure!

Read Isaiah 55:9 in your Bible

JOIN THE ADVENTURE

Every weekend SATTAR picks out a board game for us to play as a family. Sometimes it is a strategy game and sometimes it is just a game of chance. Sometimes I win. Sometimes Milo wins. When we start the game we never know who is going to win but we always have a lot of fun playing together.

Imagine if I decided that I didn't want to play unless I knew for sure I was going to win. If I did that I would just end up sitting on the sideline watching everyone else play and have fun. I would miss out on all the fun, even if I didn't win that time.

A life spent following Jesus is a life of adventure. We never know for sure what will happen. Hard and challenging times will come. We may even lose sometimes. But we can be sure that God is always with us and that he is on our side. Read this Bible Verse from Hebews 11:1

"Faith is being sure of what we hope for. It is being sure of what we do not see."

We can faith that God has a great adventure for us in life. But we have to choose to get in the game and not sit on the sideline. Make the choice today to follow Jesus and live out the adventure of faith he has for you!

What does it mean to be a Christian?

Read Philippians 3:8-9 in your Bible

Jesus took the punishment for our sin when he died on the cross. When we believe this we become right with God. This is a gift we receive by trusting in Jesus. There is no more sin between us and God. Now we can make a choice daily to follow God. We do this by spending time with God. By reading the Bible and praying. We grow closer to God by obeying his Word in the Bible, and we let Holy Spirit show us how God wants us to grow. This is the adventurous life of a Christian!

DE-CODER KEY

Use this key to de-code the Bible verses throughout the book

A 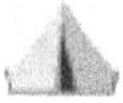	B 	C 	D 
E 	F 	G	H 
I 	J 	K	L 
M 	N 	O 	P 
Q 	R 	S 	T 
U 	V 	W 	X 
Y 	Z 		

About the Author

Allison Reimer loves stories and has been using them to teach children about Jesus for over 25 years through her local church. She is also author of *My Faith Life Journal* and the developer of www.myfaithadventures.com

When she is not teaching and writing she likes to hang out with her husband and two kids on their hobby farm in Manitoba, Canada.

The Perfect Companion to My Faith Adventures!

Full of fun Bible-based activities, **My Faith Life Journal** helps children grow in their faith in Jesus, develop godly character and discover that God has an awesome plan for their life.

ORDER ONLINE

www.myfaithadventures.com

www.ingramcontent.com/pod-product-compliance
Lightning Source LLC
Chambersburg PA
CBHW050440010526
44118CB00013B/1618